*Street Fighting and Other Past Times*



'By measuring the distance, we come home.'
Raymond Williams, *Border Country*

PARTHIAN

A CARNIVAL OF VOICES IN INDEPENDENT PUBLISHING

**Dai Smith** was born in the Rhondda in 1945. His writing has encompassed history, biography, essays and criticism. He was Series Editor of the Library of Wales and Chair of the Arts Council Wales and was made a CBE for services to arts and culture in Wales in 2016. He currently edits the Modern Wales Series and was Chair of the Dylan Thomas Prize. Smith is the author of four fictional works: *Dream On*, *What I Know I Cannot Say*, *What Lies Beneath* and *The Crossing*. His memoir *Off the Track* was published in 2023 and followed by *Measuring the Distance* – a mix of deceitfully plain reportage, fictive history and fictional forays into the past – in 2025. *Street Fighting and Other Past Times* is his debut collection of poetry.

# Street Fighting and Other Past Times

Dai Smith

PARTHIAN

Parthian, Cardigan SA43 1ED
www.parthianbooks.com
First published in 2025

ISBN 978-1-917140-72-0
Cover design by Syncopated Pandemonium
Typeset by Elaine Sharples
Proofread by Harper Dafforn
Printed and bound by 4edge Limited, UK
Published with the financial support of the Books Council of Wales
British Library Cataloguing in Publication Data
A cataloguing record for this book is available from the British Library
Printed on FSC accredited paper

# CONTENTS

*For Norette, Again and Always.*

# Twilight

*Thanking Peter Finch*

'Only poetry
Left then
For you
To do,
I mean,'
He said.

And said
That truly
He meant
To say
That, against
Any misgivings.

I said
'Adjective-laden!
Epithet-heavy!
Sig-nif-i-cant!
Gravid verse!
Not me!'

'Mmm,' he said, ars-poetically,
'Snip the choke of tendrils.
Scissor all succulent stems.
Let pungency rot till luscious
Fruits swell to fall and plop
Bursting open line by line.'

So,
Cracked gourds resound,
And seeds spilled late
Scatter over the ground
To shrivel or germinate.
A late beckoning
From fading light.

# Welsh Water

Against our lean-to's house wall
Set squatly on brick columns
A white ceramic sink agape
                    and
Plumb above its plughole
                    a
                Brass tap.

The tap's Janus head would twist
Just the one way left for water
To flow lead-piped mountain to tank
                    gushing
Gravity dropped, violently cold
                    To splash.

Coming down from summer's play
Grass stained and prickled by heat
T-shirt soaked with ludic sweat
                    I'd
Slake a daylong thirst
                    and
                Drink direct.

Strained upwards on tiptoes.
Mouth clamped over the spout
Sucking down channelled streams
                    till
Glacial melt swelled to make
                    taut
                Belly's drum.

One such day of dry-mouthed swelter
Cup or glass scorned to swallow
Fast the quick pulse of ice water
I
Gulped and felt its squirm
wriggle
Hawked out

Into the Belfast box's whirl
A comma in the swirling pool
Coppery gleamed and flickering
alive
A-shiver in its shared surprise,
a snake.

I had tasted its metallic otherness
A presence slithered tap to gob
And filled a glass now to rinse
memory
To scramble its netherworld message
through
Tepid spit.

Then, scooped elastic in a tumble
A-writhe within glassy walls
The snake curled in confinement
under
My hand, over the meniscus curve
before
waterfalling
Earthwards.

# Taking His Breath Away

*'Fan dan! Mynufferni!*
*Bobol bach o Bala!'*

Gouts of chesty wheezing
Flecking his blistery lips, spit
Pebble dashing his stubble.

And me, a dented tea tray
Held in two hands, to make
Ding-click-ding stir the air
For him to suck its passing
Down into a pulmonary void
Beyond his gaping mouth.

He lay propped up by tick pillows
Striped pyjama top open above
His undulating chest's sea curl.
Medical aids in smug attendance
A pink rubber-bulbed glass inhaler
Besides the chasuble for his sputum.

In Coronation Year no oxygen cylinder
To help inflate his latticed lungs,
To fool the delicate fretwork
Into thinking Pneumo could be crowned
By the salvation of an NHS
Created to rid us of life's thorns.

I watched, helpless, and ever unforgiving
Of what he'd been suffered to endure.
His defiant shouted Cymraeg a bridge
Back to his lost faraway places
Whilst his wrinkled hands intertwined
Gripping the stigma of his ending.

# English Civil Wars

From the high mountain he took the turf,
Dug out in the squared-off clodges he spaded
Geometrically across the tilted water meadow
Alien within a sog of bulrushes and tip clinker.
It took him all one Sunday to slice and carry
Bucketed clumps turn by turn down to the dirt
Oblong patch set forlorn above our backyard.

Fat earth worms wiggled like baby penises,
Pink and purply wrinkled, stitch-stitching
The loamy soil of wedges crested with tufts,
Grassy crewcuts trembling atop the sods
Transplanted as a checkerboard pocket lawn.
He watered its joins twice a day to fuse together
A grafted green shape for us to sit on and play.

As, when that mid-century summer came,
So did my cousin and I, both watched over
By the sisters who had married as the war began
Our English fathers: mine present, his still away.
Mine, a lung collapsed from Army bivouacking
And a leg spliced into shards by flying glass,
A long limping haul to fetch and lay a lawn.

*

Home is the Sailor
Home from the Sea
Laden with Gifts
For Him and for Me

*

The decorated War Hero
Tanned by Singapore sun

Bicycle pumped for hours
For fetid air to inflate

The purloined life raft
Up to paddle pool size,

Just right for we two
To splash and slither

Inside its rounded rubber
Through days of holiday heat

Whilst the grass beneath us
Withered, yellowed to die.

# Dogs

When the women died
One by one, the dogs
Came to us two by two.

On mantelpieces arrogantly
They sat, twinned and haughty,
Readying to become a pack.

These spaniels are all front,
Curled over Caroline locks
But plainly plebby at the back.

Yellow eyed and black snouted,
Gilt watch-chain fobs flaunted,
Arse bottoms flatly plonked.

We know all former owners well,
This Mamgu and that Bopa,
That Auntie and this Nana.

These creamy dogs have pride of place
As was and is their right –
Not ornaments, household deities.

In a backroom two are shiny black.
Gold flecks enriching the colour,
Sleek to touch, compact and dark.

Sometimes, overnight I think, moving
They might miscegenate and breed.
And so, in hope, I look away.

# My Father's Scarf

He took scant
comfort
from clothes.
Second-hand
suits his lot.
Shirt's collar tight,
frayed threads,
immaculate aprons,
washed-out whites.
Feathered blood
and squished guts
vanished overnight.
Clean-shaven,
carbolic-soaped,
his shop image
a front. He only
wore it to 'go out',
a pre-war scarf –
cobalt blue,
checkered white,
*to be washed*
*as silk*. A loose,
whispery necktie
soft around
his throat.

A gift he'd cherished
I wear for him.

# Street Fighters

The gloves came laced together at Christmas.
A rite of passage, as if by osmosis it seemed,
For all the eight-year-old boys in the street.

We emerged, as one, from our terraced houses:
Gloved up, short trousered, dapped feet pawing
The cold uneven ground, one by one, in waiting.

Men: fathers, uncles, older brothers, neighbours
Through a fug of festive cigar smoke eyed us up
And down, to pair us off in a 'fair fight'.

Weight was reckoned for more than height.
So, me short and stocky, he slight and tall,
In the bellied-up street-middle, squaring off.

Roger held his shiny gloves high, stood erect.
I crouched, my hot fists scrunched in leather.
Both apart, until a nudge knocked us together.

His toy fisticuffs clipped and scraped my face
Blow on blow unreturned, out of my reach
As I flailed away at the air heavy between us.

Seconds out for the next round of pain
And then, reddened into tears after that,
A collier spun me around at the last

To whisper 'Get above. Punch down.'
On the rise of the rollercoaster street
I smacked oncoming Roger as he rose

To be halted by my own surprise.
Popping bam bam his beaky nose
Smashing his strawberried mouth open
To end it.

# Slosh

*i.m. Sergeant Philip John Price (1945-1972)*

Not a thump or a crack
Not a smack or a crump
But from the high-held paddle
A whale-backed rounders bat
A scuffed-to-softness tennis ball
Hit ever skywards with a slosh.

Stood up or down the long street
Never missing, ever, first choice
For any pick-up sides, he would
Dismiss, fast or slow, any ball thrown
And make his loping oval run around
Our circle of salute for his slosh.

I see 'Slosh' still, tow haired, blonde
Whey faced, steady, quite without guile,
Possessed of the stance of a 'Natural'
A sinewed power in ten-year-old arms
To conjure up effortless Home Runs
Magicked from the air by one slosh.

To run home free.
No stopping him, ever.
Except the once.

## Fundraiser

Stella alfresco before the enchanted women
teasing out bids for tabled trinkets, more
than they should; the men yet underground.

Stella shimmering amongst the floral pinafores,
her green and gold wraparound cinched tight,
her bunched black curls a-tangle.

Stella dancing to the crackled gramophone,
pear-shaped earrings swaying,
a film star, stellar, fallen amongst us.

*

The salesman parted the crowd from back
to front, self-entitled, to ask how much
for the earrings, and, sensing the smile

he heard in the whispered 'Not
for Sale', waved all that away to flutter
a crinkled white fiver in front of her,

plucking the teardrop lights
from her lobes, laying down
fabled banknote and bought baubles,

encircling the tremble of her waist
Mr Gable swung his Ava into a dance,
cheek to cheek with his better buy.

*

The nightshift came home as one man,
moving towards the backs of the gaping women,
Tin waterjacks clanging, all in blackface.

The music of the nightshift made a dissonant din,
one only ended at the table's clear notation
of promises deferred and betrayal underway.

Amongst the women, in silence,
the nightshift halted for one to tear
apart the promissory paper,

to scatter, from a dirtied pay-packet,
a grime of silver coins.

## The Contender

*i.m. Billy Eynon (1893-1980)*

One-eyed Billy Eynon
An old man crouching
Whistling lefts and rights
Missing me by fractions.
Laughing.

Bantamweight Contender
Soup-kitchen Legend
Scrapping for pennies.
Driscoll'd thumbed him
Half blind.

In our back kitchen
My teacher, a God
Showing me moves
To feed the children.
Like he did.

# Gang Warfare

The weapons were all readily to hand:
stones from unmade roads, bricks fallen
to hurl upwards in a biblical storm, down
into the ranks of their protected phalanx,
a testudo of lofted dustbin lids advancing.

What madness crazed such scholarly gangs
of children intent on harm and evil,
sectarianism the DNA of our street-war games,
as we stoned each other year on year
until a boy was struck to the ground and
death followed.

# The Aftermath

A new boy, in awe of all,
Its difference and distinction,
Begowned masters and corridor laws,
Behaviour way beyond my reach
In that cocksure town by the sea.

A neophyte, I kept a distance
From intimacies I could not share,
Of place and people, accented
High and low, away from ours.

A Shoni, prickly and uneasy,
No welcome here, or even queries
Until the sick history man known
As Chick came back to teach.

A Taff, one he helped to ground
By asking where from and why,
Knitting together misplaced steps
For memory to allow forward paths.

His forehead was caved in, dented.
His bonce was pancake shiny, yellowed.
His skull was pitted pink, cratered.
His cranium a wartime memento mori.

His stick sidestepped wasted leg muscle,
His fleet skills destroyed by soldiering
In fields alien to the athletic grace shown
In the games once lit bright by his star.

Out of the hand, with a smile and a nod,
Onto my desk a Boys' Enclosure Pass,
Cardiff v Llanelly, Cardiff Arms Park.
'Watch the Scarlets' Full Back,' he'd said.

The red-jerseyed white-numbered 15
All fluid motion, film-star handsome,
A field gun boot, a brick wall tackler,
Bynea born, Terry Davies, A Local Hero.

How astute Chick's feel for the downcast
How gracious his raising up my head
To quickstep faltering teenage dubiety
With my first vision of common greatness.

Chick, Mr Trevor Davies, irreplaceable
For the brave time he had left to spend
Teaching us in the aftermath of that war
Of the gift of the thing war could not kill.

# Attendance

After the swim, all rubbed dry,
You knelt to towel the sand
From between my curling toes.

I did not merit such Magdalene care
Nor the love you would shower upon me.
A photograph X-rayed our destiny.

## Nobody's Perfect

'I have blemishes,'
        She confessed.
'Nobody's perfect,'
        I comforted,
The allusion lost.

'No, real blemishes,'
        She insisted.
'Can't see them,'
        I lied,
Turning away.

'Look, one knee
Bigger than the other.'
And raised her skirt
For me to looksee
And admire.

'Look, this bluey dot
Is no beauty spot.'
'Coal dust,' she said.
Silica, a childhood graze
A semaphored ellipsis on a knee.

'Not blemishes at all.'
        I said.
'Markers of what and why,
Significations of History
Semiotics of Industry
Inscriptions of Landscape.'

'You what?' she asked.
'Look, I'm all askew.'
Standing, her legs now akimbo,
At a slant held before me,
Her skirt hitched up left.

On her innerside thigh
Bone white scar tissue,
Six inches crosshatched
Where clumsy clamping
Pulled together the dig

For the fatty tumour,
Too blood mapped
To stitch back.
Blemished, maybe.
But not so to stop

The kisses I planted
All the scar's livid
Puckered length,
Loving, and more,
Her blemishes away.

# Tasmanian Devil

At the top
of her arse,
the left cheek,
was clearly stamped.
Faded dusky pink,
an outline map:
Tasmania.

That hidden mark,
a raggedy imprint:
not for franking
not for posting
or being licked
by any other sticky
tongue
than mine.

## Rifts

What you see with some despair
As your wrinkles, the rifting of age,
I see as ley-lines, the tracks of a train
Taking us back to the rills of love,
Its spate of passion etched for keeps.
No rifts between us, my lady,
Only the cartography of love.

# Saying Goodbyes

You see our time as running out.
I see all the days we've gathered
In our memory cache for forever.

You wonder when it will be Goodbye.
I counter with all the Goodbyes we said
And never intended for any cashing in.
Each Goodbye a mere caesura,
Each one a poised parenthesis,
Each a bridge between we made.

# Personal Archive

Open the boxes, go on!
Let fly the stoppered spirits.
Forgotten letters, forsaken ideas.
The memoranda of a lifetime
    All gone.

Open the boxes, no GPS
To guide you bodily back
To lost lands of once being.
Only the stench of dreams
    As remains.

# Top Man

Imperious Victorian cast in bronze
His masterplan unfurled for his eyes
Looking down, no need for other sight:
Docks, rail umbilical from pits to ships,
  Imported Brigades of Labour directed
            To risk.
Venture Capital, all homegrown extracted,
Finances the blood price of caisson harbours
Mastering tides to secure congregated vessels,
His coal bearing missionaries to far continents
  To dominate.

  Still his Barry statue lunges
  Outside Palladian Offices
  Still his Llandinam selfie brags
  Of Arcadian Origins
  And we are dupes yet
  To let them fool us
      Still.

      Gwerin?
  This Imperial Cymro
  Never a Peon
  Ever a Conquistador.
      Our Lord.

# Nuclear Reign

*Bristol Channel*

After the rain, the twinned Holms lurked,
The Flat one for beaching, the Steep for hiding,
Stepping stones, both, to launch mayhem.
These Viking lairs, a signal warning for all
To fear still what cannot be controlled
When blood and fire burn up the water,
All settlement upended then in chaos
Beyond any human sense or bearing.

In the Channel, shat out from alimentary Docks,
Collier vessels queued up for quick release,
Sailing across the globe to stain Edens
Yearning to become carbon-rich paradisos.
A century of steam coal delved and defecated
To make the World's axis turn, giddy drunk,
Spinning through blind hopes of restful ease.
The seeds of death in our hot, polluting gifts.

Across the channel, solar rays twist sacral mist
Curls from fast rivered Combes. The watery
Levels on the near horizon clearing to unveil
The twinned domes poised ready as lids
To house and fire up the nuclear sun –
Our vanishingly simple panacea for former ills.
Unless its gritty black rain funnels down one day
As our unheeded final destruction.

# En Bretagne

### i. La Toussaint

On the Day of the Dead the living appeared,
Bothersome amongst the endless quiescent rows,
Disturbing all the ordered gravities of matter,
Discounting the inscribed numbers
Of days ended.
They carried flowers of forgetting, fresh tributes
To raise phoenix-like in live memory those lost,
As if by celebration they might raise their dead
Into a frisson of life.

Marigolds burned orange bright, heather scented
The air earthy, honouring, not mourning,
The lives taken away through disease,
By age, accident or the murder
Of the sea.
In the graves, perilously clifftop-clung,
Weeping mariners keen in muted anguish
Their silent rebuke of this comforting,
This lack of grief.

### ii. Au Bord de la Mer

In the rented gîte, on that Breton shore,
We huddled together all that night,
Listening
As down below chairs slammed chests and
Tables crashed cupboards, though we knew
All doors were locked, all windows shuttered.

Against the bedroom door, we put the wardrobe.
Against the rattled glass panes, a heavy blanket
Soundmuffling.
Beneath the floor voices shrieked into the wind
Whose howl made lights flicker, on-off, at will
And we knew the ghosts we had feared had come.

In the seeping halflight of a broken day
We dared to stir, to look downstairs,
Creeping,
Wooden boards flinching at our tread,
To find everything in order, all as before.
Our skeletons at the table, the sea at our door.

# Swimming with the Women

At dawn the overarm strokes cleave the waves
In a unison of elemental water and damask air.
Cold burning ice splinters prick rippling backs,
Liven a trio scything to and fro across the bay.

Dry-robed, bobble-hatted, gloved, coffee-bottled,
The women materialise in a chatter at the edge.
To paddle and dip and shriek in sixes and sevens,
Bobbing, bumping bodies, sea-walking, incessant unity.

Unspoken discord slaps in and out over the tide's motion,
Nothing remotely wild to hear or see, just the seethe
Of aqueous resentment, ebb and flow, from sea to shore,
From swimmers to waders, from seaweed to plankton.

# The Lost Boys

*6 February, 1971*
*Scotland 18 Wales 19*

Outside the North British in the Edinburgh cold
We crowded close together, calling for our heroes.
'We've got JPR Williams in Our Team,' we sang
On an endless loop: 'The Best Team in the Land.'
And on down every hallowed and numbered jersey,
From 15 to 1, through all the disciples, name by name,
Worshipping Barry, Hailing Gerald, Adoring Gareth.
None much older, some younger even, than us then.
Their dart and deeds already memory incised in us.
Murrayfield their Elysium, Victory our Ambrosia.
Bobble-hatted, we cheered.

We made them our gods, these youthful Titans,
Sprung from our parental loins, and the birthplaces
We knew and thought then would be forever eternal.
They had left our terraced rows for fields of praise
And common streets for screens, and onto pages
As if their imprint was of ourselves in reverso form.
Intaglioed cameos, crafted profiles from that history
We scarcely noted in its going, even as it left us
To be a past time they would now always inhabit
Momentarily, as in a team photo on the hotel steps.
Dazzled, we cheered.

The night was splintered by flashbulb coruscations
Silhouetting in rows above us, the After Dinner squad,
Tight together as one body assembled to win by right
Against brute force and raw muscle by wit and belief,

A decade of confident revengeful assertion to come.
Welfare Wales, from pitheads to pedagogy, swaggering,
All griping tension gone, all tortuous resentments eased
To a fluency of being, inexplicable without our history.
A grizzled, black-tied prop, a survivor, oldest here by far,
From that known distance fixed us with a basilisk stare:

'Oi, Boys'
he said,
'Fuck off home.'
Blinded, we cheered,

# Downfall

The copper beech tree shudders, quakes
Before the storm, its branches lowered,
Its shaggy bison's head bowed down.
            Submission.
The spread-out leaves oxblood veined,
Readied to bleed, waiting to snap and fall.
From first to last fated to meet this end.
            Buffaloed.
Top-heavy, overloaded, the weighted tree
Bends the knee, as it must, dipping head
To prairied earth in a final exhaling of breath.
            Vanished.

# Trading Places

From the upstairs balcony of the Globe
From the windows of the projection booth
A wavering cone of light tumbling down
Over stalls to the screen, a whirling palette
Of amber and noir, mingled half tints
Of filmic chiaroscuro, to entrance knowing
Minds and peering squints of cineastes.

Until Jamie Lee Curtis, in a blink of the eye,
Unveiled her bodily litheness in a teasing strip
Cloaked by the darkness of shadow play.
Ocular confusion turned to audible dismay,
Cat-calling patrons, visually outraged by deprivation,
Moaned aloud to startle, to wake the projectionist
Stumbling to switch dimmed bulb power electric to Max.

And *son et lumière*
Lit Caravaggio flesh
For the illuminati
To cop an eyeful.

# In Transit

He/She/They doppelgangered in the panes
As slow passing trains slid double-glazed
Mirroring windows past one another
Reflecting quicksilvered glances
A mercurial quiver of self-attraction.
More Narcissi than Actaeons, Diana.
            So kiss their arses.

From the high cutting above slum backyards
Orwell stared down to telescope reality to image:
A Prole, sacking apron, her bare red arm stuck
Up a blocked downpipe, her eyes locking with his,
And no agency, only her desolate captivity in the rain
To star in an end-of-the-pier literary show.
            The self-fingering tosser.

In heat through the open frames of lowered windows
Sunblinded Larkin took in the jostle on platforms
Of dullards, the celebrants of a gathered bovine herd,
Unwitting participants in enforced feeble unities
Best viewed from afar in a cerebral shudder,
An induced spasm of distaste coming to hand.
            The fucked-up voyeur.

Cultural Exchange jolts outside the halted DART.
From disappeared Wales a billboard poster poem
Platforms Idris' bereft plea to escape from 1926;
His words 'Let's go to Barry Island, Maggie fach'
Saccharined by line and wash to timelessness,
All bitterness sweetened: History become Myopia.
            Lethe by the Liffey.

# On the Half Shell

My first was on the seafront, Rhyl.
Just a fleck of snot.
The Sixties.

Upstairs on the table, Montmartre.
Gagging after three.
The Seventies.

Trying Rockefellers, Mèze.
Tricked; I vomited.
The Eighties.

Titillated by heat, Sète.
Too saucy by far.
The Nineties.

Quick-shucked flat ones, N'Orlins.
Bang out of order.
The Oughties.

Prim and proper, Whitstable.
A native politesse.
The Teens.

Would it ever happen for me?
That fusion of jism and brine
Of which I'd read and envied
In the telling of sated others.
Their looks nothing to laud,
Gulping live slipperiness,
A swallowing-down, that's all.

# All Shucked Out

Above the black disc of an estuarine lough,
In darkling Galway, it happened at last.
We stopped the car as the rain-pittered waters
Spread flat below a twisting cinch of road.
Only two of us sheltering in that dank barroom,
The smoulder of a banked-up peat fire smoking
For mid-morning warmth against autumnal damp.

No one present to be seen to serve, so we called out.
From the gloom, floating, the apparition of a girl
Freckled pale, languorously hesitant, intent on listening
As we spoke too fast in our removed and distant accents.
An Irish coffee against the cold; for me a pint of Guinness
With half a dozen local oysters, freshly harvested, inevitable.
They came on a pewter plate, antic unhinged shells upturned,

Loosened, lying back in pearly pools, ready to be raised up.
Never such luscious opalescence atop the shrinking fronds,
A surrender of willing, nacreous fleshiness, a tangy insolence.
Each plumped and virginal bivalve an unrepeatable savour,
Until the next in line; mouth and palate awash with succulence
Before its qui-viveness was flooded by the smart of saltwater
Rushing on down, throat to stomach, all spent, to drown there.

Alive to my pleasure, you urged me to lust for more,
Another six laid out for my attention, by the girl
Who stood aghast to stare at my wanton gluttony.
I asked if she would like to try one.
Her mouth snapped shut, and then opened wide, defiant:
'No such thing will ever pass my lips so long as I so live. Ta.'

Tant pis for her.
Bully for us
Between sheets
In Connemara
That night.

# The Dark Arts: Lost and Found

## (i) Taking the Piss

*Minutes of Mountain Ash Urban District Council,*
*17 November 1948:*

'The UDC exercised
its discretionary legal powers
to
provide entertainments.
They contacted
Arts Council Great Britain
about
an art exhibition
or
sculpture in the area,
and,
asking for Arts Council
advice
and
support.'

*12 January 1949:*

'Huw Wheldon,
the
Welsh Regional Director
for
the Arts Council,
attended and asked them
to support
a
marionette show
and
the Luton Girls' Choir.'

### (ii) Lifesaver

'At Porth County
I was the only person,
at that time,
to have
taken an exam
in art.

At home, where
my father was unemployed
since 1926, nothing
but support.
In fact, I felt I had
the whole community
in support.

I wanted to make pictures
of a size and subject
they could put on a wall
and want to see.

I left school in 1946:
a scholarship
to Cardiff College of Art
then National Service in Egypt,
teaching art to fellow servicemen.

To London – Royal College
of Art. No grant aid.
My grandfather gave me
twenty pounds.
His lifesavings.'

Charles Burton
(b. Treherbert, 1929)
Painter

### (iii) Enrichissez-Vous

Etonians live and work
in a rich environment.
Our view of education
celebrates
the creative, physical, spiritual
as much as
the intellectual.
Career choices take many
along
traditional paths:
Law, the City, the Professions
but
also, these days,
in greater numbers now
to
the media, the creative arts
and
entrepreneurial adventure.

Eton College.
Prospectus, 2013.

### (iv) Two Times Two

'Any fool can see that two times two make four, but it takes a real capacity to stretch it to five, or better still, six or seven.' – **Aneurin Bevan (1897-1960) in conversation.**

You can't tell them
that they will come
        to this.
Not really.

You didn't ever listen
so why should they
        to this.
Not really.

What is forever real
always never comes
        to this.
Yes, really.

# Autodidact

*i.m. Nicholas Evans (1907-2004)*

When he retired from work
He set himself to work again.

He commandeered the cold back bedroom
And set up the easel he'd left at fourteen.

No paints or brushes touched in fifty years
As locos were instead shunted and stacked.

On primed and squared canvas or boards
He built up paint with rag-bound fingers.

Faces, bodies, clothes and houses, the weather,
Grimed in dirtied greys and unrelenting blacks.

With his thumbs he gouged out eyes, planed cheekbones,
Limned the creased thrust of a nose, the gash of a mouth.

He paraded the innocent faithful and pilloried the damned
As corpses, both dead and living, an ossuary of skulls.

He worked every day into the nights still left to him
To testify to whatever sorrow and redemption had been

Or were yet, and steadfast he prayed to his Lord that
Soon all might come to its end, above and below ground.

One year, for his wife's birthday, as penance and in praise,
He painted, in a glow of colour, a single vase of flowers.

# Rhondda Painters:

### (i) Ernie

In conversation like a geyser
Spluttering, gouting, warming
Up to a boil, then a crescendo,
Unstoppable gush of words,
Denunciatory, loving, enraged
At injustice, snobs, all authorities.

The imagery disturbs – coffined houses,
People haunted, tapeworm rivers and
Mole-blind cars take us off all maps
Of perspectives and cosseting colours.
A cascade of rockets bursts all bounds.
His vision; his once and Promised Land.

### (ii) Charlie

The somnolence of cats, the biography of chairs.
Pock-marked pine-ends, sun-pitted shadows.
What is concave made convex in a prism
Of insight, coolness a chromatic grace note.
Feline brushstrokes invoke the mundane,
Coax out meaning, transmute the ordinary,
Alchemise leaden existence to an aura of life.
Line and colour his route to what is numinous.

His tiny tiddly drinkers decant from the club,
Wend sideways home from Sunday boozing.
The little coal train's dirty steam puff pillows
The bedfellow black and green of fields and tips.
Between wars, a storm comes to shake and whirl
Manikin armies of snowballing innocents to flight.
In the maw of the pit's take all life is a sacrifice,
In the spaces of the streets life can be reclaimed.

# Assignments

'Every Good Wish/Yours in Sport/All the Best'.
The maladroit naffness of fumbling encounters
Briefly consummated over book-strewn tables.
Just the once: Signatures for kudos and cash.

Some dedicatees, as if by *lèse-majesté*, only sign
For themselves, no coy personalisation granted,
Self-gratitude their calling card of proclaimed self,
Their jerky monikers more piss-proud than priapic.
Being singled out of the crowd is all; once possessed,
Possessiveness becomes the owner's hallmarked trait.
Collected hierarchies calibrated by bestowed fame
Swell and groan on shelves tumescent with renown.

> 'For Dai in Dai Country'
> > Scribbled Al.

> 'While Seasons Twine'
> > Poeticised Ron.

> 'Michael Foot'
> > Scrawled Footie.

> 'For Dai from Gower'
> > Fantasised Gore.

> 'Before We Go On'
> > Warned Mailer.

*'Sláinte!'*
Cheered Famous Seamus
  Who
Bored by repetition
    Snarled
'South!'
When handed
    His
  'NORTH'.

To pluck a copy down, to read my courted assignees
Induces unease at an ardent past of bibliophiliac pleas.
Such authentication through autographs, nothing less
Or more than an onanistic lust for coveted simulacra.

Anorak, I'll no longer play that fruitless game, or
Not unless some 'Meet You Under the Clock at Five'
Signals the coded sincerity of some desired signer.
Then, at least, at last, an improper assignation made.
One to be kept.

## After The Appreciation

*For Chris Williams (1963-2024)*

When you leave
Say more than, remembering,
You knew him.
Say more than, mourning,
You cared.

Think more that
He is now where
Memory never sleeps;
Where the passing
Seas of Life
Run on through
Tides of love
Too deep
To fathom
Too diurnal
To forget.

# This Mongrel Breed

When the Future
Did not arrive
They just invented
Whatever they could.
(Cymru for Wales)

When linguistic fluency
Stuttered and stalled
They just changed
The Rules of the Game.
(Speakers not Learners)

When the political Map
Blushed populous red
They highlighted green
Territory bottom to top.
(Grass not Class)

When leftover people
Withdrew from voting
They altered the compelling
To make it just compulsory.
(Populace in Dissolution)

When everything devolved
Nosedived out of sight
They just doubled down
Fast in a consensual tailspin.
(Constitutional Parachuting)

When schooled language drills
Drifted to playground anarchy
They policed the neglected
Precincts of impure academies.
(Numbers only Count)

When the Past of Wales as was
Proved too embarrassing now
They fudged Public Memory
Dismissed the burden of meaning.
(Identity trumps Culture)

When lived experience was forgotten
Complexities lost in Civic Dementia
They branded the Present as Cymric
Burying Welsh remains in the grave.
(Colonised Internally)

When the Future was subtitled
They ensured the Past was mute
Only trivia escaped the Network
Banners flapped silent in the wind
(Mouths stuffed with Mold)

When I cried out in anger
'Over my dead body!'
They made especially for me
One more coffin of secrecy.
(The Alone to the Alone)

*

No Brit here
Nor Cymro either
Will ever lie.
Just Pure Welsh.
(Mongrel History)

*

When the dust had settled
New voices were heard,
History inflecting each note,
Learning to sing in harmony.
(Cymru fydd Wales)

When choral unity came overall
Discord was its needed virtue,
Dissonance its courteous exchange.
Tribal solipsism a misplaced fart.
(Dialectic for Wales)

# Notes

**Slosh:** Philip 'Slosh' Price, a Welsh Guardsman, was one of nine people murdered, seven civilians and two soldiers, on 21 July 1972, Bloody Friday, when an IRA bomb, one of nineteen set that warm afternoon, exploded in Oxford Street Bus Depot in Belfast. The IRA said that the fact that there were civilian fatalities was 'a matter of deep regret'. Philip is buried in Trealaw cemetery, mid-Rhondda, just a slosh away across the river from Ely Street, Tonypandy.

**Top Man:** Lord David Davies (1818-1890), 'Top Sawyer', girdled mid-Wales with railways, deep sank Rhondda pits, had Barry Docks built to export their immense output. Grew fabulously rich. In his youth, for his father's lumber business, he was a top sawyer, cutting timber from above whilst another worked in the sawpit below, and so himself avoided the lungfuls of sawdust which fell down on a non-family member. He was, apparently, proud of that.

# Acknowledgements

To Peter Wakelin for use of his categorization of the paintings of Charles Burton, and to Charlie for the found poetry in his memory.

To Susie Wildsmith at Parthian for straightening the kinks and supporting the better lines.

And to Richard 'Top Man' Davies for giving an octogenarian newcomer a poetic chance.

PARTHIAN

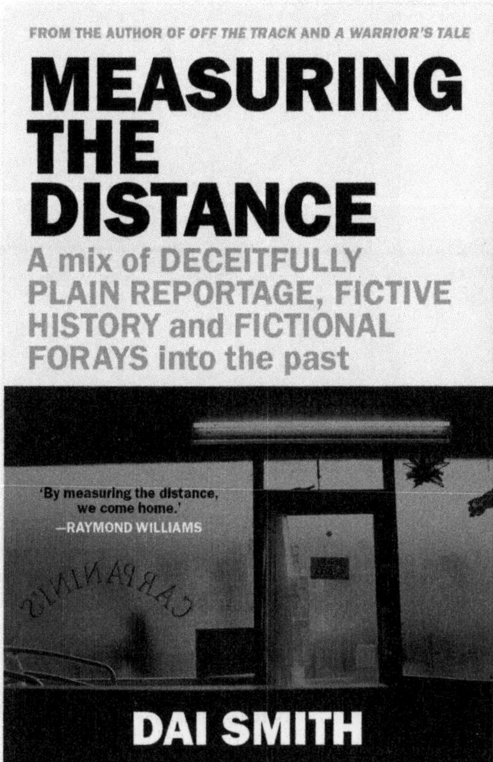


# Measuring the Distance

## Dai Smith

ISBN 978-1-917140-39-3
£10.00 | Paperback

One of Wales's most successful interpretive voices of a generation casts his mind back to the preceding decades to offer a retrospective take on the legacy of the Labour party in Wales in a genre-defying work written in Dai's inimitable signature style.

For readers who are interested in both the pre- and post-devolutionary cultural landscape of Wales, it is a crucial addition to the canon of Welsh writing in English, crowning and celebrating a life filled with enriching work at the coalface of Welsh culture.

**As he reaches eighty Dai Smith comes out swinging with *Measuring the Distance.***